museum **highlights**

CONTENTS

The Rhinebeck Panorama (detail), *c.*1806
This spectacular view invites us to imagine that we are viewing London from a balloon above the Thames. The anonymous watercolour was discovered lining a barrel of pistols in Rhinebeck, New York, in 1941.

FOREWORD

Welcome to the Museum of London.

I am delighted that you have chosen to visit today. Before you begin your journey from London in 450,000 BC to the present day city (and beyond) let me explain a bit about this museum.

The Museum of London tells the ever-changing story of this great world city and the people who live here. Our galleries, exhibitions, displays and activities give you a sense of the vibrancy that makes London such a unique place.

So much has happened in the capital that we can barely contain it within this building. During your visit you will encounter Roman Londinium, the London of Shakespeare's day, the enormity of the Great Fire in 1666, the splendour of an Edwardian Pleasure Garden, the Suffragette's struggle for the right to vote, the devastation of London during the Blitz, and the swinging 60s – as well as ideas about the future of this magnificent city and so much more. Not to mention the world-famous iconic residents who have walked London's streets.

We have a passion for London; now that you've visited we hope you too will share this passion.

Sharon Ament
Director of the
Museum of London

Woodcut from the
Chronicle of England, 1497

NVM·AVGG
DEOMARTICA
MVLO·TIBERINI
VSCELERIANVS
C·BELL·
MORITIX·
LONDINIENSI
VM
RIMVS

**Fragment of a Roman
building inscription**
This is the earliest known
mention of London recorded
on a Roman inscription.

A MUSEUM FOR LONDONERS

The Museum of London was opened by Her Majesty Queen Elizabeth II on 2 December 1976. The first new museum building to open in London since the Second World War, it attracted 370,000 visitors in its first six months and instantly acquired a reputation for excellence: 'no other museum in Britain received such all round glowing reports from our visitors', said *The Good Museums Guide*.

The new institution brought together two older museums: the London Museum and the Guildhall Museum. Both had lost their premises during the war, so uniting them was an inspired step. From its beginning, the new Museum saw itself as 'not simply of or about London, but also for London'. Its mission then and now is to play a part in the lives of all Londoners, 'to inspire a passion for London'.

The collections and the permanent galleries tell the story of London's development as a city over hundreds of thousands of years: from prehistoric settlements in the Thames Valley, through the founding of 'Londinium' by the Roman army, to the great world city that London is today. How did London come to be such an extraordinary place? Who were the Londoners who lived here in the past? What does the future hold? The Museum explores all these questions and more. It is a truly remarkable story.

Union (Horse with two Discs), 2001
This intriguing sculpture by Christopher Le Brun stands at the Museum's entrance. The two discs are said to stand for night and day, and the horse symbolises journeys.

THE MUSEUM'S COLLECTIONS

In 1976 the newly opened Museum boasted of its 'half a million objects'. Since then numbers have grown, and many nationally important items have entered the collections.

Today, the Museum has around one million items in its core collection, plus an additional six million 'finds', some in fragments dug up as part of archaeological excavations. All human life is represented in these objects, from a Roman 'bikini' worn by a female athlete, to a suitcase carried by a Turkish Cypriot man when he arrived in London as a refugee. The collections are constantly growing as archaeological digs unearth new discoveries; and the Museum gathers objects from today's London, as a record of life in the twenty-first-century city.

**Face of a woman,
3600–3100 BC**
Reconstructed from the
skull found in a burial at
Shepperton, scientific
analysis of the bone showed
that the woman had died in
her thirties and probably far
from her birthplace.

**Daggers from the Thames,
2000–1500 BC**
Many daggers of flint, bronze
and iron have been found in
the river. The representation
of a dagger made of bone (left)
is particularly unusual.

**Iron dagger and sheath,
6th century BC**
While this dagger blade
from the Thames at
Mortlake was probably
imported from central
Europe, its banded
bronze sheath is the work
of a British armourer.

Cast bronze swords, 1100–800 BC

A small selection of the many leaf-shaped swords dredged from the west London Thames. Some may have been lost in local skirmishes; others were probably gifted to the river.

Bronze looped palstave axe, 1400–1200 BC

Cast bronze axe from the Thames at Richmond. Such axes were probably used to clear local woodland for the laying out of riverside fields and settlements.

Bronze pegged spearhead, 1420–1100 BC

Large spearhead from the Thames at Hammersmith. Remains of its apple wood shaft survived in the socket, allowing it to be scientifically dated.

Bronze coins of Cunobelin, AD 10–40
Cunobelin (Shakespeare's Cymbaline) was a British tribal leader who ruled parts of southern Britain in the first century AD. His death provided the Romans with a pretext for invasion in AD 43.

Blue glass bead, 2nd–1st century BC
This blue glass bead with yellow and white trailed decoration from the Thames at Richmond probably formed part of a prized necklace.

Bronze-bound wooden tankard, 1st century BC/AD
This splendid tankard from the Thames at Kew has a capacity of over two litres (four pints). Such vessels were probably passed round at communal feasts.

ROMAN LONDON

The Roman occupation of Britain heralded the foundation of London as a settlement, following the annexation of Britain as a province of the Roman Empire in AD 43. With the new settlement growing on both sides of the Thames (in what is now the City and Southwark), Londinium became the communication and administrative hub and a trading emporium that served the burgeoning province.

The first Londinium was totally destroyed in AD 60, during the uprising of the tribes led by Queen Boudica, but was quickly rebuilt so that by AD 100 it had become the largest and most influential city in the province. At its height, it boasted a thriving port, a large forum and basilica, public baths and a fort which housed soldiers working for the military administration. The amphitheatre, religious complexes and temples served the spiritual needs of Roman Londoners, a cultural mix of diverse nationalities from around the empire.

The Museum's Roman collections, among the finest in the country, have been much enriched in recent years as the spate of new office building in London has enabled archaeologists to unearth both unique treasures as well as evidence of everyday life.

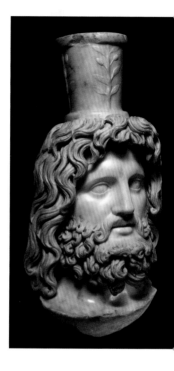

Head of Serapis
Marble head of the Romano-Egyptian god of the Underworld. Wearing a corn measure on his head to symbolise agricultural fertility, he came from a group of sculptures from the Temple of Mithras.

Novelty oil lamp
Small ceramic lamp depicting a human foot wearing a sandal. The lamp, an early import into Roman London, once had a wick burning in the hole in the big toe.

Ribbed bowl
Cast blue glass bowl. Minerals, such as cobalt, produced the prized deep blue during the glass-making process and such vessels were expensive imports for the luxury market.

Perfume bottle
Barrel-shaped container for perfumed oils. Made by Frontinus Sextinus in the Rhineland provinces of the Roman Empire, the vessel would have been a fancy container for a highly prized import.

Mercury with ram and tortoise
The marble messenger of the gods sits on a rock, holding a money-bag. The ram symbolises fertility and the tortoise, through music from tortoise-shell lyres, the eternal happiness of the afterlife.

Bacchic group
Marble scene showing a group of revellers supporting the central figure, a drunken Bacchus. As god of wine, the inscription below praises Bacchus for 'giving life to wandering mortals'.

Venus figurine
Pipeclay image of the goddess of love and fertility. Made in France, this would have been bought as payment to the gods for fulfilling a vow to be lucky in love.

Figure of Hercules
Known for his Herculean labours, which included the slaying of a lion, this bronze Hercules is shown wearing the lion skin as the symbol of his success.

Hairpin

Long bone pin, terminating in a female bust with an ornate coiffure. Such pins were needed to hold the hairstyles of the day in place. Similar pins are shown around the top of the head.

Comb and manicure set

Ornate bone comb and bronze manicure set used for personal hygiene. The manicure set consists of implements for keeping nails manicured, for removing excess hair and for mixing and applying make-up.

Military belt fittings

Bronze belt set, finely decorated with spiral motifs and animal heads. Its style indicates a wearer who was probably a high-ranking German military official working for the late-Roman administration.

Necklaces
One of these necklaces, made from amber beads from the Baltic, is still strung on its original thread while the other, made of gold wire links, includes emeralds from Roman Egypt.

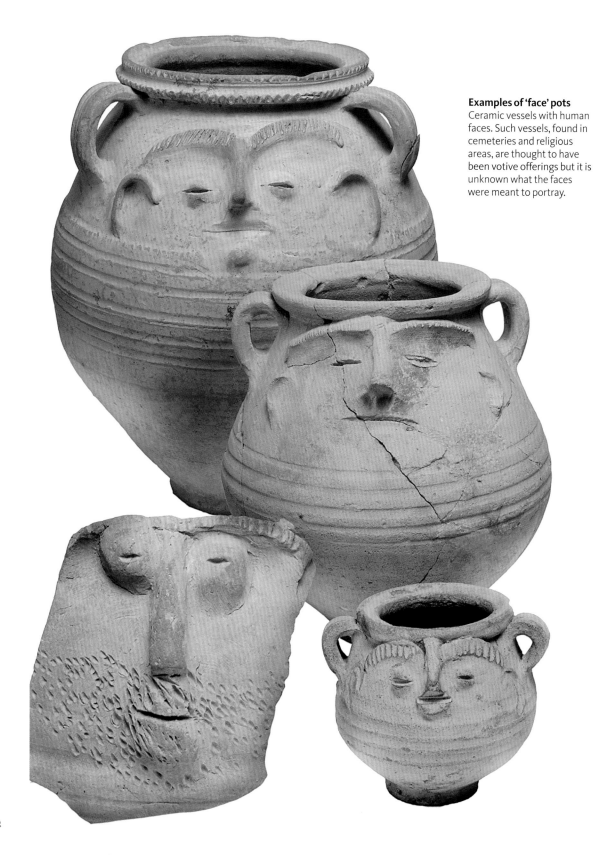

Examples of 'face' pots
Ceramic vessels with human faces. Such vessels, found in cemeteries and religious areas, are thought to have been votive offerings but it is unknown what the faces were meant to portray.

Canister and strainer
Silver-gilt cylindrical container decorated with figures of men and animals. It has an internal silver perforated strainer, probably used for infusing herbs or drugs as part of the Mithraic rituals.

Engraved depiction of Pegasus
Banded agate intaglio, for use as a seal in a signet ring, depicting the mythical winged horse. It was found in a jeweller's shop, destroyed in the Boudican rebellion of AD 60.

Coin of the Emperor Hadrian
Gold aureus, one of a hoard found hidden under the floor of a substantial building in Fenchurch Street. Such coins, never in everyday circulation, would have been used for large business transactions.

Word die
Basalt die with pigment-filled letters that correspond to the numbers on normal dice. The type of word-game is unknown but 'Italia' (Italy) was equal to a throw of six.

MEDIEVAL LONDON

The Museum's medieval collections illuminate a long period of history, from the Anglo-Saxon settlement in the fifth century, through Viking raids and the Norman Conquest of 1066, to the splendour and bustle of London under Tudor rule, and the dramatic consequences of Henry VIII's dissolution of the monasteries.

This was the period when London's merchants and craftsmen consolidated their position as privileged citizens, banding together in crafts, guilds and parishes to create a system of self-government that still survives today, particularly through the office of the Lord Mayor of London, which dates back to 1189.

London grew rich as a trading centre, its population reaching a peak of perhaps as much as 100,000 by 1300, only to be decimated by the Black Death (bubonic plague) which raged through Europe in the 1340s. The city's appearance also changed. Saxon houses were simple and built from wood, wattle and daub. Typical medieval houses were tall and narrow, with the upper storeys overhanging into the street. The main landmarks in medieval London were churches, their towers and spires creating a distinctive skyline. Tallest of all was St Paul's Cathedral, a colossal building and the largest in medieval Britain.

Gilded silver brooch, early 500s
Although made in southern England this brooch shows strong Scandinavian influences. It was found in the grave of a young Saxon woman to the south of London.

Silver penny, c.880
This penny was minted in London around 880. One side shows the head of Alfred the Great and the other a monogram of 'LVNDONIA' – the medieval Latin for 'London'.

Copper-alloy, gold and garnet brooch, mid 600s
Found in a grave during excavations in Floral Street, Covent Garden, this brooch would have belonged to an aristocratic Anglo-Saxon lady. Floral Street lies in the heart of the early Saxon settlement of Lundenwic.

Viking weapons, early 1000s
In the late 900s and early 1000s London was under attack by the Vikings. At one point they pulled down London Bridge. These Viking weapons were found near the Bridge.

Face pot, early 1300s
Is this the face of a medieval potter? It appears on a jug made in Kingston to the south of London. Face pots were very popular at this time.

Medieval pottery
Large quantities of pottery vessels were imported into London. They were made in the area around London but also in France and northern Europe.

Glass beaker, about 1300
Intended for wine, this fine Venetian beaker is decorated with coloured enamel. The shield with a blue wolf shows the arms of the Wolfsberg family who held land near Augsburg in southern Germany.

Paternoster bead, early 1500s

This bead symbolises the transience of life. Carved with a woman's head on one side and a 'death's head' on the other, it was used as an aid to prayer.

Annunciation altarpiece, c.1500

The 'wings' of a triptych altarpiece depicting the Angel Gabriel with the arms of Westminster Abbey (left); and the Virgin Mary with the arms of Abbot George Fascet (right).

WAR, PLAGUE AND FIRE 1550s–1660s

By the 1550s London was a wealthy city, but an uneasy one. The last Tudor monarch, Queen Elizabeth I, held power but religion still divided loyalties, and England remained vulnerable to invasion or insurrection.

This was the London that William Shakespeare knew. The Museum's collections include items related to the Rose Theatre, which stood on the south side of the river at Bankside from 1587 to 1605. Many of the greatest playwrights of the day had works performed at the Rose, and William Shakespeare acted on its stage.

By the 1640s ideological tensions had split England into warring factions. London became the stage for some of the Civil War's most traumatic events, in particular the execution of King Charles I, who was tried for treason and beheaded in public on Tuesday 30 January 1649. The watching crowd is said to have let out a low moan.

London from Southwark, c.1630 (detail)
This is the earliest known painted view of London. It shows Old London Bridge, the Tower of London and the spires of the City churches.

The Great Fire of London, 1666
The Great Fire was the most destructive fire England has ever seen. After five days, 13,200 homes had gone and four-fifths of the City was destroyed

Fireman's helmet, late 1600s
The City churches kept fire-fighting equipment for emergency use. This helmet, painted 'BB' and 'GB', was probably used by the parish of St Botolph and St George Billingsgate.

Ring and Brooch, early 1600s
These jewels form part of the Cheapside Hoard, a cache of 400 gems and other precious objects discovered by workmen in 1912.

EXPANDING CITY 1660s–1850s

The years following the Great Fire heralded the start of a new chapter in London's story. The city expanded on the ground and its influence spread across the globe. London became capital not only of a 'united kingdom' but also of a vast empire. In size and population, wealth and power, there had never been a city like it.

All aspects of London grew phenomenally from 1666. Printing presses multiplied and Londoners developed an appetite for newspapers, ideas and debate. London was also Britain's largest manufacturing centre, noted particularly for its specialist products such as watches and scientific instruments. By the 1850s Queen Victoria was on the throne and London housed a Great Exhibition, promoting England as the 'workshop of the world'. By now London had long overtaken Paris as Europe's largest city. It was a busy and chaotic place, a confident city that thrived on free enterprise. People were drawn to London from all parts of the world and the massive new docks handled unprecedented quantities of cargo.

This London was a city of amusement as well as hardship. Pleasure gardens, theatres and music halls thrived in the capital, alongside workshops, warehouses and prisons.

Nelson's sword of honour, 1798
The Corporation of London presented this honorary sword and the Freedom of the City to Admiral Lord Nelson in 1800 to mark his victory at the Battle of the Nile.

Panorama of London, detail of Old London Bridge, 1749
Samuel and Nathaniel Buck
This engraving, one of five, forms part of a long panorama of the north bank of the Thames from Westminster to the Tower of London.

Duelling Pistols by Toms, c.1810
These flintlock duelling pistols belonged to a captain in the Hackney Volunteer Riflemen, a militia established in London during the Napoleonic Wars.

Commemorative gold ring with miniature medals of Prince Albert and Queen Victoria, 1840
Six dozen of these rings were made for Queen Victoria's marriage.

Gold and enamel cased watch made by Jefferys and Jones, c.1781
Many costly and intricate London-made watches were exported to Europe, Turkey and the colonies.

The Cockpit,
**William Hogarth,
1759**
Cockfighting was
London's most
popular sport
at this time.
The venue in
Hogarth's
engraving is the
Royal Cockpit
near St James's
Park. The central
figure is the blind
aristocrat, Lord
Albemarle Bertie.

The Idle 'Prentice Executed at Tyburn,
William Hogarth, 1747
Taken from the 'Industry and Idleness'
series, this engraving shows the
hanging of Tom Idle for highway
robbery. London's public executions
drew enormous crowds and shops
would close for the occasion.

Southwark Fair, **William Hogarth, 1733**
Hogarth's engraving depicts a typical
London street fair. Entertainers of
various kinds can be seen, including
actors, acrobats, street musicians and
a magician. Gambling and petty crime
are also evident.

OPPOSITE:

Papier-mache souvenir album of the Great Exhibition, 1851
In a spectacular temporary exhibition building in Hyde Park, more than 100,000 works of industry of all nations were put on display.

Model of the Great Exhibition, 1851, by J. Paige
In this model, the two naves of the exhibition have been shortened. The actual building was three times the length of St Paul's Cathedral.

The Blackett Family Dolls' House, c.1760
This 'baby house' was a gift to Lady Anne Blackett from her husband Edward. The Blacketts were a wealthy provincial family who had London connections through Edward's involvement in commerce and politics.

Anne Fanshawe's dress, c.1751
This spectacular dress is made from brocaded silk, woven in Spitalfields. The dress was made for Anne Fanshawe, the daughter of Crisp Gascoyne, a merchant who became Lord Mayor of London in 1752.

OPPOSITE:
***Eastward Ho!*, August 1857, Henry Nelson O'Neil**
Soldiers are shown boarding a ship at Gravesend, leaving to fight in the 'Indian Mutiny', the first Indian war of independence.

***Home Again*, 1858, Henry Nelson O'Neil**
Here, in the companion work to *Eastward Ho!*, it is one year later and the same soldiers are returning home, being greeted by family and friends.

THE VICTORIAN WALK

The look and feel of London around 1900 is vividly evoked in one part of the Museum's galleries. The shop fronts, fixtures and fittings in 'the Victorian Walk' are all original and come from buildings demolished in the 1960s or 1970s.

   The shops include a pub, a tobacconist's, a barber's, a chemist, a grocer's, a tailor's and a pawnbroker's. There is also a bank office and a recreation of the showroom of the London glass manufacturers, James Powell & Sons, who produced their famous 'Whitefriars' glass from a working glasshouse in the City of London until the 1920s. The glass inside the showroom was all made by Whitefriars.

OPPOSITE:
The Barber
The barber's shop has original fittings from several shops, including Pottle's in Upper Street, Islington. The copper towel heater dispensed steaming towels to soothe the skin after a close shave.

The Tobacconist
The shop fittings in this reconstruction are from Redford's tobacconist shop in Clerkenwell. The wooden Highlander and Blackamoor figures advertised the sale of Scottish snuff and American tobacco.

PEOPLE'S CITY 1850s–1950s

By the 1850s London was the world's wealthiest city. But success had come at the expense of its people. Overcrowding and sanitation problems divided the city, whose rich and poor lived in separate worlds.

As the social divide widened, so concerns deepened and the need for action became more urgent. A new system of local government began to tackle the city's massive problems of poverty, housing and health. The Suffragette demand for 'Votes for women!' was one of many campaigns that brought political debate on to London's streets.

Technology quickened change as Londoners became accustomed to electricity, telephones, motor vehicles and moving pictures. A housing boom created new suburbs, enabling London to spread its boundaries and form the outline shape of Greater London as we know it today.

By 1939, one in five of the British population lived in the

OPPOSITE:
The Arrest of Emmeline Pankhurst, 1914
This photograph shows the Suffragette leader Emmeline Pankhurst being arrested outside Buckingham Palace as she attempts to present a petition to the King in support of female suffrage.

Behind the Bar, 1882,
John Henry Henshall
Here, the artist paints women and children in a working-class pub, a sight deplored by those who campaigned against alcohol. Pubs were a centre of community life in Victorian London.

capital. London remained the hub of a global empire, receiving a constant flow of goods and people from around the world. But two world wars left Londoners with a terrible reminder that their city's fortunes could fall as well as rise. 'Blitzkrieg' bombing in the winter of 1940–41 left thousands dead and buildings in ruins.

WEALTHY

WELL-TO-DO

COMFORTABLE

POOR & COMFORTABLE (MIXED)

POOR

VERY POOR

SEMI-CRIMINAL

Sections from the Map of Poverty, 1886–1903
Charles Booth's survey into life and labour in London mapped the social character of every street in the city. The colour coding represents degrees of poverty and wealth.

Gold shoes, c.1925

These shoes were made by Ignazio Pluchino. Ignazio was born in Sicily and moved to London in 1900, where he established his business in Chelsea making beautiful shoes for wealthy clients.

Wedding dress made from Indian sari silk, 1931

The fabric was presented to the wife of the headmaster of Highgate School by the Thakur Sahib of Rajkot, to thank her for caring for his son, who died from tuberculosis whilst at the school. In 1931 the fabric was made up into a wedding dress for her daughter.

Marshall & Snelgrove lift panel, 1930s

This Chinese-style panel was part of a lift interior in Marshall & Snelgrove's Oxford Street department store.

Model Y Ford 8 car, 1936
The Model Y Ford 8 was a London-made car, one of the first to roll off the assembly line at Ford's newly built Dagenham factory in 1932. It went from drawing board to production in just 10 months.

Selfridges lift, 1928
The American Gordon Selfridge opened his Oxford Street store in 1909. By the 1920s Selfridges was the most glamorous department store in London. Its gilded bronze lift was installed in 1928.

***Women in a Shelter*, 1941, Henry Moore**
Londoners in underground air-raid shelters, as seen by the artist Henry Moore. He described the shelters as a 'huge city in the bowels of the earth...I was fascinated. I went back again and again'.

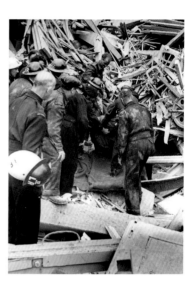

Budge Row, 1944
A rescue party at work after a V-1 flying bomb exploded. The man pulled out of the rubble was one of several rescued alive.

War damage in the City of London, 1940–44
These photographs were all taken by two police constables, Arthur Cross and Fred Tibbs, who recorded the damage as it happened. The view on the right was taken in January 1941. The bomb had penetrated the booking hall of Bank Underground station, killing 50 people.

**A bombed bus,
9 September 1940**
This bus had been hit by
a high-explosive bomb
falling in the early hours
of the morning.

**Queen Victoria Street,
11 May 1941**
The Salvation Army
Headquarters at
Queen Victoria Street,
photographed just as the
building facade fell.

**St Paul's Cathedral,
10 October 1940**
Showing bomb damage
to the cathedral's roof.

WORLD CITY 1950s–TODAY

During the 1950s London was still recovering after its wartime ordeal. The population had shrunk and there was much to do in the way of reconstruction.

The new London that took shape in the 1950s and 1960s felt very different from its pre-war predecessor. London's old economy faltered as old firms shut up shop and the docks began to close. A youth revolution brought a new energy to London, along with a new obsession with fashion.

Above all, the faces of Londoners changed as people began to move around the world more easily, settling in a city that already had a global dimension. By the end of the twentieth century, London was a truly cosmopolitan world city, diversity at its heart.

As with all world cities, London cannot help but speculate about its future. Climate change poses challenges. How can the city reduce its carbon footprint? Where will the jobs of the future come from? Should London build higher skyscrapers or deeper tube lines? Whatever the future, this inspirational world city will never stand still.

Bill and Ben the Flower Pot Men, 1950s
Bill and Ben were two of the puppet stars of *Watch with Mother*, a children's television programme first screened in the 1950s.

Beatles mini dress, 1964
Worn by Pauline Richey when selling programmes at the premiere of the Beatles' film *Hard Day's Night* at the London Pavilion in 1964.

Mary Quant dress, 1966
Mary Quant opened her
boutique, Bazaar, in the King's
Road in Chelsea in 1955. This
dress is made of bonded
jersey, a fabric very popular in
the 1960s because it did not
crease and held its shape.

Pashmina shawl, 2008
Designed by Alexander
McQueen, the son of a
London taxi driver who
became a global
fashion name. This
print appeared on
many items in his
Autumn/Winter 2008
collection.

'Mayor's chain', 2007
Produced by Tatty
Devine, the trading
name of two former
artists who opened a
shop in East London's
Brick Lane in 2001. The
chain is a quirky version
of a traditional mayoral
chain of office.

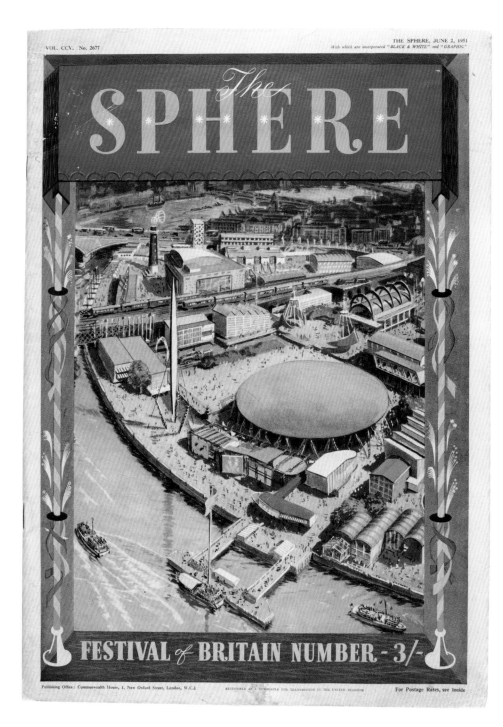

The Sphere **magazine, 1951** The cover story celebrates the Festival of Britain exhibition on London's south bank. The futuristic structures and buildings included the Dome of Discovery and the slender Skylon.

**_History Painting_, 1993–94,
John Bartlett**
The 'Poll Tax Riot' broke out
in Trafalgar Square on
Saturday 31 March 1990, as a
protest against the new tax.
The artist wanted to capture
an occasion that had historic
significance for London.

**_Spirit of the Carnival_, 1988,
Tam Joseph**
This print captures the
hostility between the police
and London's Caribbean
community which blighted
the Notting Hill Carnival
during the 1970s.

Photographs by Henry Grant (1907–2004)
Henry Grant was a photojournalist who worked in London from the 1950s to the 1980s. His entire archive of thousands of images is now held by the Museum.

Badges
A few of the 2,000 badges in the Museum's collections. These examples date from the 1960s to the 1990s. The black and gold badge is 1970s and comes from Biba, the famous London fashion shop.

**London Fields –
The Ghetto, 1994
(part)**
Part of a large
model of Ellingfort
Road and London
Lane in Hackney,
by model-maker
James Mackinnon
and photographer
Tom Hunter. The
two streets were
lived in by
squatters and
were under threat
of demolition at
the time.

**Portraits of the
residents, 1994**
These photographs by Tom
Hunter were intended to
show that the residents of
Ellingfort Road, although
squatters, had spent time and
effort on their homes. Many
had been living there for over
10 years.

THE LORD MAYOR'S COACH

'The City' is the capital's historic core, a place steeped in tradition yet ultra-modern. Today, it is famous for international finance, yet many other things happen within its square mile. People live and study there, and thousands of commuters arrive on weekdays to work in shops, sandwich bars and offices.

The Museum's most spectacular exhibit is part of the City's living tradition. The Lord Mayor's State Coach is a superb example of eighteenth-century coach building, and it is still in working order. It leaves the Museum every November to carry the newly elected Lord Mayor through the City streets in the annual Lord Mayor's Show.

The office of Lord Mayor dates back to the twelfth century. The holder is the head of the City of London Corporation and represents the City on national occasions. Since 2000, London has also had a city-wide mayor: this Mayor of London is head of the Greater London Authority, the strategic body for the whole of London.

The Lord Mayor's State Coach
The coach was commissioned in April 1757 from Joseph Berry of Leather Lane, Holborn, for the fixed price of £860. It was finished in record time and was first used in November that year.

THE LONDON 2012 CAULDRON

The London 2012 Olympic and Paralympic Games reinforced London's reputation as a global city and creative force. It became the focus of the world's attention. The city swelled with visitors and incredible sporting achievements were played out against its striking backdrop.

As midnight approached on 27 July the London 2012 Olympic and Paralympic Cauldron designed by Thomas Heatherwick was revealed. At the climax of the opening ceremony its 204 stems rose up in the centre of the Olympic Stadium in Stratford. Each stem carried a fragment of the Olympic flame in a uniquely shaped copper piece, only burning as one when they finally and perfectly nestled together.

The cauldron became an iconic centrepiece of the 2012 Games and a symbol of contemporary London. Spectacularly reimagined at the heart of the Museum, this stunning object retains a dash of magic from that extraordinary summer.

The London 2012 Cauldron
The cauldron was created by the internationally renowned Heatherwick Studio and has become one of its best-known works. Creative engineers Stage One controlled the cauldron's motion and metalworking experts Contour crafted the unique copper elements.

THE SACKLER HALL

The Sackler Hall is a space for rest and refreshment on the lower floor of the Museum. Overhead, a striking installation – made up of a 45-metre-long elliptical digital curtain and an array of large screens – presents new work specially created for the space by some of London's most exciting filmmakers and digital artists. At the north end of the Hall, a bank of computer pods enable visitors to find out more about any object on display, and to browse through our Collections Online database. To the south are changing display spaces dedicated to contemporary London, reflecting the city's creativity and the people, stories and issues that matter to Londoners today.

MUSEUM OF LONDON DOCKLANDS

If you have enjoyed your journey through London's turbulent past, then why not complete your introduction to the city with a visit to Museum of London Docklands? From Roman settlement to Docklands' regeneration, this 200-year-old warehouse reveals the long history of the capital as a port through stories of trade, migration and commerce.

Discover a wealth of objects from whale bones to World War II gas masks in state-of-the-art galleries, including Mudlarks, an interactive area for children; Sailortown, an atmospheric recreation of nineteenth-century riverside Wapping; and London, Sugar & Slavery, which reveals the city's involvement in the transatlantic slave trade. With ancient finds, unusual objects, fascinating tours and free family events, Museum of London Docklands is one of the capital's hidden treasures.

Open daily 10am–6pm (galleries begin to close at 5.40pm; closed 24–26 December)

To find out more call 020 7001 9844 or visit **www.museumoflondon.org.uk/docklands**

Museum of London Docklands
West India Quay
London E14 4AL

 West India Quay

 Canary Wharf

 Canary Wharf Pier

VISITOR INFORMATION

For general information
Telephone **020 7001 9844** or visit the Museum's website **www.museumoflondon.org.uk**

Museum of London
150 London Wall
London EC2Y 5HN

By tube: Barbican, St Paul's
By rail: Liverpool St, City Thameslink, Farringdon
By bus: 4, 8, 25, 56, 100, 25, 172, 242, 521

Be the first to know about events and exhibitions
Have details of what's on, plus special offers, sent straight to your inbox by signing up to receive our free enewsletter.
Visit **www.museumoflondon.org.uk/enews** or enquire at the information desk during your visit.

Opening hours
Daily 10am–6pm (galleries begin to close at 5.40pm)
Closed 24–26 December

Shop
The Museum of London shop has something for everyone – from super London souvenirs to perfect presents for all the family, celebrating every age and aspect of this thriving metropolis. If this wasn't enough, with over a thousand books about the city on sale, you are sure to find the right title for that last-minute gift or school project, as well as specialist and academic publications for adults and children alike. The good news is that we can also be accessed 24/7 from the comfort of your own home at **www.museumoflondonshop.co.uk**

To find out more about our products or services, including mail order and school goody bag offers, please contact us directly on **020 7814 5600** or email **shop@museumoflondon.org.uk**.

Eating and drinking at Museum of London
Our Benugo cafés offer a range of freshly made sandwiches, teas, coffees and handmade cakes, while our restaurant London Wall Bar & Kitchen serves a great menu of modern English classics plus traditional ales, fine wines and tasty cocktails. For more information about eating and drinking at the Museum, please call **020 7600 2352** or email **mol@benugo.com**, or visit **www.museumoflondon.org**

Access and facilities for visitors with disabilities
The Museum is fully accessible to wheelchair users. Please call or visit our website to find out about the services and facilities we provide that may help you during your visit.

Schools
We offer a rich programme of free sessions, video-conferences and INSET courses for primary, secondary and special schools to enrich teaching across the curriculum. See the Learning section of our website for details.

Events

There's always something happening at Museum of London. Visit our website for details of what's on or pick up a leaflet during your visit.

Group visits

With a range of exclusive tours, talks, and walks, plus discounts for groups visiting temporary exhibitions, find out how we can make your group visit a day to remember. Visit **www.museumoflondon.org.uk/groups**

Picture Library

The Museum of London Picture Library holds thousands of images illustrating the history of London and its people. An extensive range of prints are available to purchase from **www.museumoflondonprints.com** Images are available to license for editorial use from **www.museumoflondonimages.com** Please contact the Picture Library for more details on **020 7814 5612** or **5604** or email **picturelib@museumoflondon.org.uk**.

Filming

The Museum buildings and galleries provide a unique location for filming. For details of conditions and fees please contact the Press Office on **020 7814 5502** or email **press@museumoflondon.org.uk**.

Host your event at Museum of London

The Museum's venue hire facilities include daytime meeting spaces and a 230-seat purpose-built theatre. In addition, the Museum can be hired for drinks receptions for 1,000 people or the Sackler Hall for fine dining for 350 people. There is also a tranquil city garden ideal for summer parties. Please contact the sales team on **020 7814 5789** or email **venuehire@museumoflondon.org.uk**.

Supporting Museum of London

Museum of London relies on public support to ensure that we remain free. As a charity, we very much welcome a donation of £5 from every visitor who can afford it. If you would like to become a Friend of Museum of London, or perhaps introduce us to an individual, company or charitable trust who might be able to assist us, please contact the Development Office on **020 7814 5591** or email **development@museumoflondon.org.uk**.